PENGUIN BOOKS

RUSKIN BOND'S BOOK OF VERSE

Ruskin Bond's first novel, *The Room on the Roof*, written when he was seventeen, received the John Llewellyn Rhys Memorial Prize in 1957. Since then he has written a number of novellas, essays, poems and children's books, many of which have been published by Penguin. He has also written over 500 short stories and articles that have appeared in magazines and anthologies. He received the Sahitya Akademi Award in 1992, the Padma Shri in 1999 and the Padma Bhushan in 2014.

Ruskin Bond was born in Kasauli, Himachal Pradesh, and grew up in Jamnagar, Dehradun, New Delhi and Shimla. As a young man, he spent four years in the Channel Islands and London. He returned to India in 1955. He now lives in Landour, Mussoorie, with his adopted family.

RUSKIN BOND'S BOOK OF VERSE

PENGUIN BOOKS

An imprint of Penguin Random House

PENGUIN BOOKS

USA | Canada | UK | Ireland | Australia
New Zealand | India | South Africa | China | Singapore

Penguin Books is part of the Penguin Random House group of companies
whose addresses can be found at global.penguinrandomhouse.com

Published by Penguin Random House India Pvt. Ltd
4th Floor, Capital Tower 1, MG Road,
Gurugram 122 002, Haryana, India

Penguin
Random House
India

First published by Penguin Books India 2007
This edition published in Penguin Books 2016

Copyright © Ruskin Bond 2007

10 9 8 7 6 5 4 3 2

ISBN 9780143426707

Typeset in Weiss by SURYA, New Delhi
Printed at Repro India Limited

www.penguin.co.in

This is a legitimate digitally printed version of the book and therefore might not
have certain extra finishing on the cover.

Contents

Nature

Childhood

Humour

Travel

Words to Live By

Haikus and Other Verses

Introduction

At the end of *The Room on the Roof*, the novel I wrote more than fifty years ago when I was still in my teens, Rusty and Kishen are trudging back to their 'home' in Dehra, and Kishen says: 'One day you'll be a writer or an actor or something. Maybe a poet! Why not a poet, Rusty?' And Rusty smiled. He knew he was smiling because he was smiling at himself.

'Yes,' he said, 'why not a poet?'

And that's where the book ends.

But not the story.

Because Rusty (read Ruskin) did become a writer; but,

having to make a living from the written word, he became
a writer chiefly of prose; for as we all know, you can't make
a living writing poetry.

But poetry remained my first love; and whenever I felt
the urge I put down my thoughts, feelings and observations
into verse form, sometimes slipping these poems into my
prose works and anthologies when my publishers weren't
looking! I have never had any pretensions to being a serious
'poet', which is why I prefer to use the word 'verse' to
describe my compositions. But I do look upon the world as
a poet would, and if there is a lyrical quality to some of my
prose it is probably because the poet in me is trying to
break free.

Ravi Singh of Penguin India thought it would be a good
idea to publish a selection from what I had written over the
years, and I thought it would be helpful for the reader if the
verses were arranged by theme, with the emphasis on Love,
Nature, Childhood, Humour, etc. Meru Gokhale has been
very helpful with the selection and arrangement of the
verses.

Perhaps Kishen (read Krishan) was being prophetic
when he said, 'Maybe a poet, Rusty...'

Is there still time, I wonder ... when we were young,
time stretched before us—an infinity of time. It is only we
who were finite.

The scruffy Kishen of the *The Room on the Roof* grew into
a successful, handsome young man. But he was barely forty
when he perished, while saving a child from drowning.

To his memory, then, I dedicate this book of verse. Perhaps he, more than any other, brought out the poet in me.

Ruskin Bond

19 February 2007

LOVE

It Isn't Time That's Passing

Remember the long ago when we lay together
In a pain of tenderness and counted
Our dreams: long summer afternoons
When the whistling-thrush released
A deep sweet secret on the trembling air;
Blackbird on the wing, bird of the forest shadows,
Black rose in the long ago summer,
This was your song:
It isn't time that's passing by,
It is you and I.

Love Lyrics for Binya Devi

1

Your face streamed April rain,
As you climbed the steep hill,
Calling the white cow home.
You seemed very tiny
On the windswept mountainside;
A twist of hair lay
Strung across your forehead
And your torn blue skirt
Clung to your tender thighs.
You smiled through the blind white rain
And gave me the salt kiss of your lips,
Salt mingled with raindrop and mint,
And left me there, where I had come to fetch you—
So gallant in the blistering rain!
And you ran home laughing;
But it was worth the drenching.

2

Your feet, laved with dew,
Stood firm on the quickening grass.

There was a butterfly between us:
Red and gold its wings
And heavy with dew.
It could not move because of the weight of moisture.
And as your foot came nearer
And I saw that you would crush it,
I said: 'Stay. It has only a few days
In the sun, and we have many.'
'And if I spare it,' you said, laughing.
'What will you do for me, what will you pay?'

'Why, anything you say.'

'And will you kiss my foot?'

'Both feet,' I said, and did so happily.
For they were no less than the wings of butterflies.

3

All night our love
Stole sleep from dusty eyes.
What dreams were lost, I'll never know.
It seemed the world's last night had come
And there would never be a dawn.

Your touch soon swept the panting dark away—
Some suns are brighter by night than day!

4

Your eyes, glad and wondering,
Dwelt in mine,
And all that stood between us
Was a blade of grass
Shivering slightly
In the breath from our lips.

But grass will bend.

We turn and kiss,
And the world swings round,
The sky spins, the trees go hush
Hush, the mountain sings—
Though we must leave this place,
We've trapped forever
In the trembling air
The last sweet phantom kiss.

5

I know you'll come when the cherries
Are ripe;
But it is still November
And I must wait
For the green fruit to blush
At your approach.

And meanwhile the tree is visited
By robber bands, masked mynas
And yellow birds with beaks like daggers,
Determined not to leave one cherry
Whole for lovers.
But still I wait, hoping one day
You'll come to stain your lips
With cherry-juice, and climb my tree,
Bright goddess in your dark green temple,
Thrusting your tongue at me.

6

Slender waisted, bright as a song,
Dark as the whistling-thrush at dawn,
Swift as the running days of November,
Lost like a dream too sweet to remember.

The Love of Two Stars

Two stars fell in love. Between them came sky
And ten moons and two suns riding high,
Before them the nebulous star-crusted Way,
The silence of Night, the silver of Day.
A million years passed, the lovers still glowed
With the brilliance and fire and passion of old;
But one star grew restless and set off at night
With a wonderful shower of hot white light.
He sped to his love, with his hopes and his fears,
But missed her, alas, by a thousand light-years.

Lovers Observed

Lovers lie drowsy in the grass,
Sunk in bracken, swimming in pools
Of late afternoon sunshine;
All agitation past, they stay totally
Absorbed in grass.

Green grass, and growing from that place
A sweep of languid arm still bare
But for a lost ladybird.
Anonymous lover brushes a dragon
Fly from his face.

Brief thunder blossoms in the air,
A leaf between the thighs is caught
And crushed. Love comes like a thief,
Crouching among the bruised and broken clover.
All flesh in grass.

Walnut Tree

The walnut tree is the first to lose its leaves,
But at the same time the fruit ripens,
The skin splits, the hard shell of the nut
Stands revealed. Yesterday (the last of August)
You climbed among the last few crumpled leaves,
Slim boy in a walnut tree, your toes
Gripping the tender bark, your fingers
Fondling walnuts, while I waited and counted,
And there were twenty-three walnuts on the grass.
We cracked them open with our teeth.
They were still raw but we could not wait:
The walnuts would age and I might grow younger!

Walnut Tree Revisited

You have ripened, since last the walnut tree
Lost its dark leaves, last autumn.
One summer intervened between your growing
And my importunity;
One summer lost,
while walnuts grew;
I too had forgotten.

We saw each other often,
But gone was the magic
Of that first encounter;
And even the tree
Gave little fruit last year.
Now it stands bare-branched
Outside the closed window,
Touched no more by feet and questing fingers,
But turning its own fingers
To the slanting winter sun.
Not one leaf left, where hundreds
Glittered like spears in the forest of September.

But I will wait until the parrots bring
Shrill portents of another spring;
(And I will love you with the same sweet pain,
If you and summer care to visit me again.)

Phantom Lover

Night unto night
When the world's asleep,
You come to me,
Our tryst to keep.
Held captive, in thrall,
As the stars look down,
Body and soul
From night unto dawn.
Silent you come
And softly you go,
Ours is a love
That none must know.

We Must Love Someone

We must love someone
If we are to justify
Our presence on this earth.
We must keep loving all our days,
Someone, anyone, anywhere
Outside our selves;
For even the sarus crane
Will grieve over its lost companion,
And the seal its mate.
Somewhere in life
There must be someone
To take your hand
And share the torrid day
Without the touch of love
There is no life, and we must fade away.

Love Is a Law

Who shall set a law to lovers?
Love is a law unto itself

Love gained is often lost
And love that's lost is found again

It's love that makes the world go round
Love that keeps us closely bound

Take this power to love away
We would be just beasts of prey

If Love should lose its hold on us
Discord would rule the Universe.

Enough for Me

Enough for me that you are beautiful:
Beauty possessed diminishes.
Better a dream of love
Than love's dream broken;
Better a look exchanged
Than love's word spoken.
Enough for me that you walk past,
A firefly flashing in the dark.

NATURE

Raindrop

This leaf, so complete in itself,
Is only part of a tree.
And this tree, so complete in itself,
Is only part of the mountain.
And the mountain runs down to the sea.
And the sea, so complete in itself,
Rests like a raindrop
On the hand of God.

Lone Fox Dancing

As I walked home last night
I saw a lone fox dancing
In the cold moonlight.

I stood and watched. Then
Took the low road, knowing
The night was his by right.

Sometimes, when words ring true,
I'm like a lone fox dancing
In the morning dew.

So Beautiful the Night

I love the night, Lord.
After the sun's heat and the day's work,
It's good to close my eyes and rest my body.
It's a good time for small creatures:
Porcupines come out of their burrows
to dig for roots.
The night-jar calls tonk-tonk!
The timid owl peeps out of his hole in the tree trunk
Where he has been hiding all day.
Insects crawl out in thousands.
The wind comes down the chimney
and blows around the room.
I'm watching the stars from my window.
The trees are stretching their arms in the dark
and whispering to the moon.
But if the trees could walk, Lord,
What a wonderful sight it would be—
Armies of pines and firs and oaks
Marching over the moonlit mountains.

The Bat

Most bats fly high,
Swooping only
To take some insect on the wing;
But there's a bat I know
Who flies so low
He skims the floor;
He does not enter at the window
But flies in at the door,
Does stunts beneath the furniture.

Is his radar wrong,
Or does he just prefer
Being different from other bats?
I've grown quite used to him:
He appeals to the paradox in me.
And when sometimes
He settles upside down
At the foot of my bed,
I let him be.
On lonely nights, even a crazy bat
Is company.

Walk Tall

You stride through the long grass,
Pressing on over fallen pine-needles,
Up the winding road to the mountain-pass:
Small red ant, now crossing a sea
Of raindrops, your destiny
To carry home that single, slender
Cosmos seed,
Waving it like a banner in the sun.

Rain in the Hills

In the hushed silence of the house
when I am quite alone, and my friend, who was here,
has gone, it is very lonely, very quiet,
as I sit in a liquid silence, a silence within,
surrounded by the rhythm of rain
the steady drift
of water on leaves, on lemons, on roof,
drumming on drenched dahlias and window panes,
while the mist holds the house in a dark caress.

As I pause near a window, the rain stops.
And starts again.
And the trees, no longer green but grey,
menace me with their loneliness.

Silent Birth

When the earth gave birth to this tree,
There came no sound:
A green shoot thrust
In silence from the ground.
Our births don't come so quiet—
Most lives run riot—
But the bud opens silently,
And flower gives way to fruit.
So must we search
For the stillness within the tree,
The silence within the root.

Listen!

Listen to the night wind in the trees,
Listen to the summer grass singing;
Listen to the time that's tripping by,
And the dawn dew falling.
Listen to the moon as it climbs the sky,
Listen to the pebbles humming;
Listen to the mist in the trembling leaves,
And the silence calling.

Firefly in My Room

Last night, as I lay sleepless
In the summer dark
With window open to invite a breeze,
Softly a firefly flew in
And circled round the room
Twinkling at me from floor or wall
Or ceiling, never long in one place
But lighting up little spaces...
A friendly presence, dispelling
The settled gloom of an unhappy day.

    And after it had gone, I left
    The window open, just in case
    It should return.

Rain

After weeks of heat and dust
How welcome is the rain.
It washes the leaves,
Gives new life to grass,
Draws out the scent of the earth.
It rattles on the roof,
Gurgles along the drainpipe
Collects in a puddle in the middle of the lawn—
The birds come to bathe.

When the sun comes out
A lizard crawls up from a crack in a rock.
'Small brown lizard
Basking in the sun
You too have your life to live
Your race to run.'

At night we look through the branches
Of the cherry tree.
The sky is rain washed, star-bright.

The Owl

At night, when all is still,
The forest's sentinel
Glides silently across the hill
And perches in an old pine tree.
A friendly presence his!
No harm can come
From night bird on the prowl.
His cry is mellow,
Much softer than a peacock's call.
Why then this fear of owls
Calling in the night?
If men must speak,
Then owls must hoot—
They have the right.
On me it casts no spell:
Rather, it seems to cry,
'The night is good—all's well, all's well.'

The Snail

Leaving the safety of a rocky ledge
The snail sets out
On his long journey
Across a busy path.
The grass is greener on the other side!
For tender leaf or juicy stem
He'll brave the hazards of the road.
Not made to dodge or weave or run
He must await each threatening step
Chancing his luck
Keeping his tentacles crossed!
Though all unaware
Of the dangers of being squashed
He does not pause or flinch—
A cartwheel misses by an inch!—
But slithers on,
Intent on dinner.
He's there at last, his prize—
Rich leaf-mould where the grass grows tall.
I salute you, Snail.
Somehow, you've made me feel quite small.

The Snake

When, after days of rain,
The sun appears
The snake emerges,
Green-gold on the grass.
Kept in so long,
He basks for hours
Soaks up the hot bright sun.
Knowing how shy he is of me,
I walk a gentle pace
Letting him doze in peace.
But to the snake, earth-bound
Each step must sound like thunder.
He glides away
Goes underground.
I've known him for some years:
A harmless green grass-snake
Who, when he sees me on the path,
Uncoils and disappears.

Once You Have Lived
with Mountains

Once you have lived with mountains
Under the whispering pines
And deodars, near stars
And a brighter moon,
With wood smoke and mist
Sweet smell of grass, dew lines
On spider-spun, sun-kissed
Buttercup and vine;
Once you have lived with these,
Blessed, God's favourite then,
You will return,
You will come back
To touch the trees and grass
And climb once more the windswept mountain pass.

The Trees

At seven, when dusk slips over the mountains
The trees start whispering among themselves.
They have been standing still all day.
But now they stretch their limbs in the dark
Shifting a little, flexing their fingers
Remembering the time when
They too walked the earth with men.
They know me well, these trees:
Oak and walnut, spruce and pine
They know my face in the windows
They know me for a dreamer of dreams
A world-loser, one of them.
They watch me while I watch them grow.
I listen to their whisperings,
Their own mysterious diction;
And bow my head before their arms
And ask for benediction.

Butterfly Time

April showers
Bring swarms of butterflies
Streaming across the valley
Seeking sweet nectar.
Yellow, gold, and burning bright,
Red and blue and banded white.
To my eyes they bring delight!
Theirs a long and arduous flight,
Here today and off tomorrow,
Floating on, bright butterflies,
To distant bowers.
For Nature does things in good order:
And birds and butterflies recognize
No man-made border.

Dandelion

I think it's an insult
To Nature's generosity
That many call this cheerful flower
A 'common weed'.
How dare they so degrade
A flower divinely made!
Sublimely does it bloom and seed
In sunshine or in shade,
Thriving in wind and rain,
On stony soil
On walls or steps
On strips of waste,
Tough and resilient,
Giving delight
When other flowers are out of sight.

And when its puff-ball comes to fruit
You make a wish and blow it clean away:
'Please make my wish come true,' you say.
And if you're kind and pure of heart,
Who knows? This magic flower might just respond
And help you on your way.
Good dandelion,
Be mine today.

Night Thoughts

This mountain is my mother,
My father is the sea,
This river is the fountain
Of all that life may be...
Swift river from the mountain,
Deep river to the sea,
Take all my words and leave them
Where the west wind sets them free.
So, piper on the lonely hill,
Play no sad songs for me;
The day has gone, sweet night comes on,
Its darkness helps me see.

Wild Is the Wind

Wild is the wind tonight,
Deep is the thunder,
Lightning across the sky
Splits it asunder.
Witches will ride tonight,
Ranging the sky,
Wizards will cast their spells—
Great men will die.
Who'll be my guide tonight,
Starless the sky;
Who'll brave the demons
Now riding so high.
I'll take the road alone,
I'll reach my goal;
Witches and wizards
Must yield to man's soul.

The Whistling Schoolboy

From the gorge above Gangotri
Down to Kochi by the sea,
The whistling-thrush keeps singing
That same sweet melody.

He was a whistling schoolboy once,
Who heard god Krishna's flute,
And tried to play the same sweet tune,
But touched a faulty note.

Said Krishna to the errant youth—
A bird you must become,
And you shall whistle all your days
Until your song is done.

These Simple Things

The simplest things in life are best—
A patch of green,
A small bird's nest,
A drink of water, fresh and cold,
The taste of bread,
A song of old,
These are the things that matter most.
The laughter of a child,
A favourite book,
Flowers growing wild,
A cricket singing in a shady nook.
A ball that bounces high!
A summer shower,
A rainbow in the sky,
The touch of a loving hand,
And time to rest—
These simple things in life are best.

A Bedbug Gives Thanks

I'm a child of the Universe
Claimed the bug
As he crawled out of the woodwork.
I've every right
To be a blight.
To Infinite Intelligence I owe
My place—
Chief pest
Upon the human race!
I'm here to stay—
To feast upon their delicate display,
Those luscious thighs,
Those nooks and crannies
Where the blood runs sweet.
No, no, I don't despise
These creatures made for my delight.
A kind Creator had my needs in mind...
I thank you, Lord, for human-kind.

CHILDHOOD

Sweet Dolly

Sweet Dolly, you're the girl for me,
Kind Dolly, I shall always see
You climbing in your father's garden,
Picking apples off a tree,
Sorting out the rosy ones
And giving them to me!

Boy in a Blue Pullover

Boy in a faded blue pullover,
Poor boy, thin, smiling boy,
Ran down the road shouting,
Singing, flinging his arms wide.
I stood in the way and stopped him.
'What's up?' I said. 'Why are you happy?'
He showed me the nickel rupee-coin.
'I found it on the road,' he said.
And he held it to the light
That he might see it shining bright.
'And how will you spend it,
Small boy in blue pullover?'
'I'll buy—
I'll buy a buckle for my belt!'
Slim boy, smart boy,
Would buy a buckle for his belt
Coin clutched in his hot hand,
He ran off laughing, bright.
The coin I'd lost an hour ago,
But better his that night.

Little One Don't Be Afraid

Little one, don't be afraid of this big river.
Be safe in these warm arms for ever.
Grow tall, my child, be wise and strong.
But do not take from any man his song.
Little one, don't be afraid of this dark night.
Walk boldly as you see the truth and light.
Love well, my child, laugh all day long,
But do not take from any man his song.

View from the Window

I'm in bed with fever
but the fever's not high.
Beside my bed is a window
and I like looking out at all
that's happening around me.
The cherry leaves are turning a dark green.
On the maple tree, winged seeds spin round and round
There is fruit on the wild blackberry bushes.
Two mynah birds are building a nest in a hole—
They are very noisy about it.
Bits of grass keep falling on the window sill.
High up in the spruce tree, a hawk-cuckoo calls:
'I slept so well, I slept so well!'
When the hawk-cuckoo is awake, no one else sleeps
That's why it's also known as the fever bird.
A small squirrel climbs on the window sill.

He's been coming every day since I've been ill,
and I give him crumbs from my tray.
A boy on a mule passes by on the rough mountain track.
He sees my face at the window and waves to me.
I wave back to him.
When I'm better I'll ask him to let me ride his mule.

Cherry Tree

Eight years have passed
Since I placed my cherry seed in the grass.
'Must have a tree of my own,' I said—
And watered it once and went to bed
And forgot, but cherries have a way of growing
Though no one's caring very much or knowing,
And suddenly that summer, near the end of May,
I found a tree had come to stay.
It was very small, a five months' child,
Lost in the tall grass running wild.
Goats ate the leaves, a grasscutter's scythe
Split it apart, and a monsoon blight
Shrivelled the slender stem…Even so,
Next spring I watched three new shoots grow,
The young tree struggle, upwards thrust
Its arms in a fresh fierce lust
For light and air and sun.

I could only wait, as one
Who watches, wondering, while Time and the rain
Made a miracle from green growing pain...
I went away next year—
Spent a season in Kashmir—
Came back thinner, rather poor,
But richer by a cherry tree at my door.
Six feet high, my own dark cherry,
And—I could scarcely believe it—a berry,
Ripened and jewelled in the sun,
Hung from a branch—just one!
And next year there were blossoms, small
Pink, fragile, quick to fall
At the merest breath, the sleepiest breeze...

I lay on the grass, at ease,
Looked up through leaves, at the blue
Blind sky, at the finches as they flew
And flitted through the dappled green,
While bees in an ecstasy drank
Of nectar from each bloom, and the sun sank
Swiftly, and the stars turned in the sky,
And moon-moths and singing crickets and I—
Yes, I!—praised night and stars and tree:
A small, tall cherry grown by me.

Kites

Are you listening to me, boy?
I am only your kitemaker,
My poems are flimsy things
Torn by the wind, caught in mango trees,
Gay sport for boys and dreamers.
My silent songs. But once I fashioned
A kite like a violin,
She sang most mournfully, like the wind
In tall deodars.

Are you listening? Remember
The Dragon Kite I made one summer?
No, you are too young. A great
Kite, with small mirrors to catch the sun
And eyes and a tongue, and gold
Trappings and a trailing silver tail.
A kite for the gods to ride!
And it rose most sweetly, but the wind
Came up from nowhere,

A wind in waiting for us,
My twine snapped and the wind took the kite,
Took it over the flat roofs
And the waving trees and the river
And the blue hills for ever.
No one knew where it fell. Boy, are you
Listening? All my kites
Are torn, but for you I'll make a bright
New poem to fly.

I Was the Wind Last Night

I was the wind last night.
I vaulted the river and swam seven mountains.
And turned aside the tall trees guarding the valley.

I caught glimpses of you through the window as I
    wandered around the little house.
They wouldn't let me in; too cold a wind!
I hung about listlessly, afraid to call too loud.
Then like a weary man limped homewards over the sleeping
    mountains

When will I learn the value of stillness?

Tigers Forever

May there always be tigers, Lord.
In the jungles and tall grass
May the tiger's roar be heard,
May his thunder
Be known in the land.
At the forest pool, by moonlight
May he drink and raise his head
Scenting the night wind.
May he crouch low in the grass
When the herdsmen pass,
And slumber in dark caverns
When the sun is high.
May there always be tigers, Lord.
But not so many that one of them
Might be tempted to come into my bedroom
In search of a meal!

Evening by the Fireside

Boy by the fire dreaming
Baby sleeping
Mother nodding, knitting
Father reading
Wood crackling, spitting
Wind in the chimney humming
Old house creaking
Small mouse squeaking
No one speaking...

Baby waking!
Boy hungry
Mother grumbly
Father rumbly-bumbly
Baby shrieking!
Old house shaking
Small mouse squeaking
Wind in chimney howling
Everyone shouting, scowling
Baby *yowling*!

Don't Be Afraid of the Dark

Don't be afraid of the dark, little one,
The earth must rest when the day is done.
The sun may be harsh, but moonlight—never!
And those stars will be shining forever and ever,
Be friends with the Night, there is nothing to fear,
Just let your thoughts travel to friends far and near.
By day, it does seem that our troubles won't cease,
But at night, late at night, the world is at peace.

Slum Children at Play

Imps of mischief,
Barefoot in the dust,
Grinning, mocking, even as
They beg you for a crust.
No angels these,
Just hungry eyes
And eager hands
To help you sympathize...
They don't want love,
They don't seek pity,
They know there's nothing
In this heartless city
But a kindred need
In those who strive
For power and pelf
Though only just alive!

They know your guilt,
They'll take your money,
And if you give too much
They'll find you funny.
Because that's what you are—
You're just a joke—
Your life is soft
And theirs all grime and smoke.
And yet they shout and sing
And do not thank your giving,
You'll fuss and fret through life
While they do all the living.

The Pool

Where has it gone,
    the pool on the hill?
The pool of our youth,
    when Time stood still,
Where we romped in its shallows
    and wrestled on sand,
Closer than brothers, a colourful band.

Gone is the pool, now filled in with rocks,
Having made way for the builders' blocks.
But sometimes, at dawn,
    you will hear us still,
And that's why they call this
    the Haunted Hill.

Granny's Proverbs

A hungry man is an angry man,
     Said dear old Gran
As she prepared an Irish stew
For the chosen few
(Gran'dad, my cousins and me).
But then she'd turn to me and emote—
'Don't be greedy, or your tongue will cut your throat!'
And if I asked for more of my favourite fish,
'That small fish,' she'd say, 'is better than
                                        an empty dish!'
Like Manu, she taught us to honour our food,
She was the law-giver, seeking all good.
Gran'dad and I, we'd eat what we were given
     (Irish stew and a tart)
But sometimes we'd sneak away to the bazaar
To feast on tikkees and chaat
     —And that was heaven!

What Can We Give Our Children?

What can we give our children?
Knowledge, yes, and honour too,
And strength of character
And the gift of laughter.
What gold do we give our children?
The gold of a sunny childhood,
Open spaces, a home that binds
Us to the common good...
These simple things
Are greater than the gold of kings.

On Wings of Sleep

On wings of sleep
I dreamt I flew
Across the valley drenched in dew
Over the roof-tops
Into the forest
Swooping low
Where the Sambhur belled
And the peacocks flew.
And the dawn broke
Rose-pink behind the mountains
And the river ran silver and gold
As I glided over the trees
Drifting with the dawn breeze
Across the river,
over fields of corn.
And the world awoke
To a new day, a new dawn.

Time to fly home,
As the sun rose, red and angry,
Ready to singe my wings,
I returned to my sleeping form,
Creaking bed and dusty window-pane,
To dream of flying with the wind again.

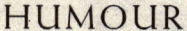
HUMOUR

Cricket—Field Placings

Long leg has a cramp in one leg,
Short leg has a cramp in two;
Twelfth man is fielding at mid-off,
Because mid-on's gone off to the loo.
As short square leg has a long leg,
Long-off has been moved further off;
Silly-point goes back to gully
Cover-point backs off a pace or two.
Everyone is thinking of the drinks' trolley
When first slip lets a catch through his fingers,
Forgetting the old ball is now new.

A Frog Screams

Standing near a mountain stream
I heard a sound like the creaking
Of a branch in the wind.
It was a frog screaming
In the jaws of a long green snake.

I couldn't bear that hideous cry.
And taking two sharp sticks,
I made the twisting snake disgorge the frog,
Who hopped quite spry out of the snake's mouth
And sailed away on a floating log.

Pleased with the outcome,
I released the green grass-snake,
Stood back and spoke aloud:
'Is this what it feels like to be God?'

'Only what it's like to be English,'
Said God (speaking for a change in French);
'*I* would have let the snake finish his lunch!'

We Are the Babus

Soak the rich and harry the poor,
That's our motto and our law;
We are the rulers of this land,
We are the *babus*, a merry band,
Under the table, or through the back door,
We'll empty your pockets and ask for more!
We are the *babus*, this is our law—
Soak the rich and harry the poor!

Do You Believe in Ghosts?

'Do you believe in ghosts?'
Asked the passenger
On platform number three.
'I'm a rational man,' said I,
'I believe in what I can see—
Your hands, your feet, your beard!'
'Then look again,' said he,
And promptly disappeared!

The Demon Driver

At driving a car I've never been good—
I batter the bumper and damage the hood—
'Get off the road!' the traffic cops shout,
'You're supposed to go *round* that roundabout!'
'I thought it was quicker to drive straight through.'
'Give us your license—it's time to renew.'
I took their advice and handed a fee
To a Babu who looked on this windfall with glee.
'No problem,' he said, 'Your license now pukka,
You may drive all the way from here to Kolkata.'

So away I drove, at a feverish pitch,
Advancing someway down an unseen ditch.
Once back on the highway, I soon joined the fray
Of hundreds of drivers who wouldn't give way:
I skimmed past a truck and revolved round a van
(Good drivers can do anything that they can)
Then offered a lift to a man with a load—
'Just a little way down to the end of this road,'
As I pressed on the pedal, the car gave a shudder:
He'd got in at one door, got out at the other.

'God help you!' he said, as he hurried away,
'I'll come for a drive another fine day!'
I came to that roundabout, round it I sped
Eager to get to my dinner and bed.
Round it I went, and round it once more
'Get off the road!' That cop was a bore.
I swung to the left and went clean through a wall,
My neighbour stood there—he looked menacing,
    tall—
'This will cost you three thousand,' he quietly said,
'And send me your cheque before you're in bed!'

Alas! my new car was sent for repair,
But my friends gathered round and said, never despair!
'We are all going to help you to make a fresh start.'
And next day they gave me a nice bullock-cart.

Foot Soldiers

'Where's Solan?' the private was asking.
'Somewhere in Tibet, I should think.'
There's a brewery there.
And it's brimming with beer,
But we can't get a mouthful to drink!'

So we route-march from Delhi to Solan
In the dust and the devilish sun,
And we're cursing away like Hades,
'Cause there ain't any ladies
To hear every son-of-a-gun!

And when we have climbed up to Solan
Our language continues profane,
For right well we know
We shall soon have to go.
Down from Solan to Delhi again.

Self-Portrait

There was an old man at Landour
Who wanted young folk to laugh more;
So he wrote them a book,
And with laughter they shook
As they rolled down the hill to Rajpore.

Portents

Spider running up the wall
Means that rain is going to fall.

Spider running down the wall
Means the house is going to fall!

In Praise of the Sausage

I like a good sausage, I do;
It's a dish for the chosen and few.
Oh, for sausage and mash,
And of mustard a dash,
And an egg nicely fried—maybe two?
At breakfast or lunch, or at dinner,
The sausage is always a winner;
If you want a good spread
Go for sausage on bread,
And forget all your vows to be slimmer.

A Nightmare

Cupid, with his famous dart,
Struck me just above the heart—
'Life' he said, 'is just a gamble,
You'll take to her without preamble.
And so there came, all bent and grey,
This withered crone, and she did sway
Backwards and forwards, as though she'd seen
The phantom lover of a dream.
She hypnotised me with one glance
And there and then began to dance,
Then tossed me in her waiting carriage
And promised me her hand in marriage.
She took me to her home in state,
And chortling, said, 'There's no escape,
I'll keep you in my empty cupboard,
You know my name—it's Mother Hubbard!
I'll feed you frogs and make you fat—
A *kofta* for my favourite cat.'

Her cat? The thing she called her darling
Was a monstrous tiger, fiercely snarling,
Its eyes were burning bright and red.
It pounced! I woke up in my bed.
No tiger lady in my cupboard...
But when I opened my front door
I found the brass plate bore
My name: Mr Hubbard.

Granny's Tree-Climbing

My grandmother was a genius. You'd like to know why?
Because she could climb trees. Spreading or high,
She'd be up their branches in a trice. And mind you,
When last she climbed a tree, she was sixty-two.
Ever since childhood, she'd had this gift
For being happier in a tree than in a lift;
And though, as years went by, she would be told
That climbing trees should stop when one grew old
And that growing old should be gone about gracefully
She'd laugh and say, 'Well, I'll grow old disgracefully.
I can do it better.' And we had to agree;
For in all the garden there wasn't a tree
She hadn't been up, at one time or another
(Having learned to climb from a loving brother
When she was six) but it was feared by all
That one day she'd have a terrible fall.
The outcome was different while we were in town
She climbed a tree and couldn't come down!
We went to the rescue, and then
The doctor took Granny's temperature and said,
'I strongly recommend a quiet week in bed.'
We sighed with relief and tucked her up well.
Poor Granny! For her, it was like a season in hell.

Confined to her bedroom, while every breeze
Whispered of summer and dancing leaves.
But she held her peace till she felt stronger
Then sat up and said, 'I'll lie here no longer!'
And she called for my father and told him undaunted
That a house in a tree-top was what she now wanted.
My Dad knew his duties. He said, 'That's all right
You'll have what you want, dear, I'll start work tonight.'
With my expert assistance, he soon finished the chore:
Made her a tree-house with windows and a door.
So Granny moved up, and now every day
I climb to her room with glasses and a tray.
She sits there in state and drinks grape-juice with me,
Upholding her right to reside in a tree.

Song for a Beetle

A beetle fell into the goldfish bowl,
Hey-ho!
The beetle began to struggle and roll,
Ho-hum!
The window was open, the moon shone bright,
The crickets were singing with all their might,
But a blundering beetle had muddled his flight
And here he was now, in a watery plight,
Having given the goldfish a terrible fright,
Ho-hum, hey-ho!

The beetle swam left, the beetle swam right,
Hum-ho!
Along came myself—I said, 'Lord, what a sight!
That poor old beetle will drown tonight.'
Ho-hum.
A beetle is just an insect, I hear,
But what if I fell in a vat full of beer?
I'd be brewed to light lager if no one came near—
(It happened, I'm told, to a man in Ajmer)—
Ho-hum, ho-hum.

With my fingers and thumb
The beetle I seized;
The goldfish were pleased!
The window was open, the moon shone bright,
I flung that beetle far out in the night,
And he bumbled away in a staggering flight,
Ho-hum, hey-ho,
Good night!

The Cat Has Something to Say

Sir, you're a human and I'm a cat,
And I'm really quite happy to leave it at that.
It doesn't concern me if you like a dish
Of chicken masala or lobster and fish.
So why all these protests around the house
If for dinner I fancy
A succulent mouse?
Or a careless young sparrow who came my way?
Our natures, dear sir, are really the same:
Flesh, fish or fowl, we both like our game.
Only you take yours curried,
And I take mine plain.

Song of the Cockroach

We are the survivors,
Crow and I,
And beetle and bed-bug and bluebottle-fly.
We dine on your refuse,
Exult in your drains,
Your poisons can't touch us—
You'll not hear us complain.
When you choke on your gases
And drown in their fumes,
All the rot in your gutters
Are the choicest perfumes.
So carry on turning
Earth's treasures to ruins,
We will sit here and laugh
While you build your own tombs.

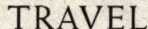
TRAVEL

Remember the Old Road

Remember the old road,
The steep stony path
That took us up from Rajpur,
Toiling and sweating
And grumbling at the climb,
But enjoying it all the same.
At first the hills were hot and bare,
But then there were trees near Jharipani
And we stopped at the Halfway House
And swallowed lungfuls of diamond-cut air.
Then onwards, upwards, to the town,
Our appetites to repair!

Well, no one uses the old road any more.
Walking is out of fashion now.
And if you have a car to take you
Swiftly up the motor-road
Why bother to toil up a disused path?
You'd have to be an old romantic like me
To want to take that route again.

But I did it last year,
Pausing and plodding and gasping for air—
Both road and I being a little worse for wear!
But I made it to the top and stopped to rest
And looked down to the valley and the silver stream
Winding its way towards the plains.
And the land stretched out before me, and the years
    fell away,
And I was a boy again,
And the friends of my youth were there beside me,
And nothing had changed.

Garhwal Himalaya

Deep in the crouching mist, lie the mountains.
Climbing the mountains are forests
Of rhododendron, spruce and deodar—
Trees of God, we call them—soughing
In the wind from the passes of Garhwal,
And the snow-leopard moans softly
When the herdsmen pass, their lean sheep cropping
Short winter grass.
And clinging to the sides of the mountains,
The small stone houses of Garhwal,
Their thin fields of calcinated soil torn
From the old spirit-haunted rocks.
Pale women plough, they laugh at the thunder,
As their men go down to the plains:
Little grows on the beautiful mountains
In the east wind.

There is hunger of children at noon, and yet
There are those who sing of the sunset
And the gods and glories of Himaal,
Forgetting no one eats sunsets.
Wonder, then, at the absence of old men,
For some grow old at their mothers' breasts,
In cold Garhwal.

Parts of Old Dehra

Parts of old Dehra remain...
A peepul tree I knew
And flying foxes
In a mango grove
And here and there
A moss-encrusted wall
Old bungalows
Gone to seed
And giving way
To concrete slabs.
A garden town's become a city
And the people faceless
As they pass or rather rush
Hell-bent
From place of work
To crowded tenement.

So change must come,
Fields make way for factories,
The trees succumb
To real-estate,
The rivers plunge
Silt-laden
To our doom…
Too late to do a thing
About it now,
For we have grown
Too many,
And the world's no bigger
Than before.
Do-gooders, don't despair!
Nature will repair
Her own, long after
We are dust.

Hill-Station

There is nothing to keep me here,
Only these mountains of silence
And the gentle reserve of shepherds and woodmen
Who know me as one who
Walks among trees.

Madman, misanthropist? They make
Their guesses, smile and pass slowly
Down the steep path near the cottage. There is nothing
To keep me here, walking
Among old trees.

A Song for Lost Friends

The past is always with us, for it feeds the present...

1

As a boy I stood on the edge of the railway-cutting,
Outside the dark tunnel, my hands touching
The hot rails, waiting for them to tremble
At the coming of the noonday train.
The whistle of the engine hung on the forest's silence.
Then out of the tunnel, a green-gold dragon
Came plunging, thundering past—
Out of the tunnel, out of the grinning dark.

And the train rolled on, every day
Hundreds of people coming or going or running away—
Goodbye, goodbye!
I haven't seen you again, bright boy at the carriage window,
Waving to me, calling,
But I've loved you all these years and looked for you everywhere,
In cities and villages, beside the sea,
In the mountains, in crowds at distant places;

Returning always to the forest's silence,
To watch the windows of some passing train...

2

My father took me by the hand and led me
Among the ruins of old forts and palaces.
We lived in a tent near the tomb of Humayun
Among old trees. Now multi-storeyed blocks
Rise from the plain—tomorrow's ruins...
You can explore them, my son, when the trees
Take over again and the thorn-apple grows
In empty windows. There were seven cities before...

Nothing my father said could bring my mother home;
She had gone with another. He took me to the hills
In a small train, the engine having palpitations
As it toiled up the steep slopes peopled
With pines and rhododendrons. Through tunnels
To Simla. Boarding-school. He came to see me
In the holidays. We caught butterflies together.
'Next year,' he said, 'when the War is over,
We'll go to England.' But wars are never over
And I have yet to go to England with my father.

He died that year
And I was dispatched to my mother and stepfather—
A long journey through a dark tunnel.

No one met me at the station. So I wandered
Round Dehra in a tonga, looking for a house
With lichi trees. She'd written to say there were lichis
In the garden.
But in Dehra all the houses had lichi trees,
The tonga-driver charged five rupees
for taking me back to the station.
They were looking for me on the platform:
'We thought the train would be late as usual.'
It had arrived on time, upsetting everyone's schedule.

In my new home I found a new baby in a new pram.
Your little brother, they said, which made me a hundred.
But he too was left behind with the servants
When my mother and Mr H went hunting
Or danced late at the casino, our only wartime night-club.
Tommies and Yanks scuffled drunk and disorderly
In a private war for the favours of stale women.

Lonely in the house with the servants and the child
And books I'd read twice and my father's letters
Treasured secretly in the small trunk beneath my bed:
I wrote to him once but did not post the letter
For fear it might come back 'Return to sender...'

One day I slipped into the guava orchard next door—
It really belonged to Seth Hari Kishore
Who'd gone to the Ganga on a pilgrimage—
The guavas were ripe and ready for boys to steal
(Always sweeter when stolen)
And a bare leg thrust at me as I climbed:

'There's only room for one,' came a voice.
I looked up at a boy who had blackberry eyes
And guava juice on his chin, grabbed at him
And we both tumbled out of the tree
On to the ragged December grass. We rolled and fought
But not for long. A gardener came shouting,
And we broke and ran—over the gate and down the road
And across the fields and a dry river bed,
Into the shades of afternoon…
'Why didn't you run home?' he said.
'Why didn't you?'
'There's no one there, my mother's out.'
'And mine's at home.'

3

His mother was Burmese, his father
An English soldier killed in the War.
They were waiting for it to be over.
Every day, beyond the gardens, we loafed:
Time was suspended for a time.
On heavy wings, ringed pheasants rose
At our approach.
The fields were yellow with mustard,
Parrots wheeled in the sunshine, dipped and disappeared
Into the morning mist on the foothills.
We found a pool, fed by a freshet
Of cold spring water. 'One day when we are men,'
He said, 'We'll meet here at the pool again.
Promise?' 'Promise,' I said. And we took a pledge.
In blood, nicking our fingers on a penknife
And pressing them to each other's lips. Sweet salty kiss.
Late evening, past cowdust time, we trudged home:
He to his mother, I to my dinner.

One wining–dancing night I thought I'd stay out too.
We went to the pictures—*Gone with the Wind*—
A crashing bore for boys, and it finished late.
So I had dinner with them, and his mother said:
'It's past ten. You'd better stay the night.
      But will they miss you?'

I did not answer but climbed into my friend's bed—
I'd never slept with anyone before, except my father—
And when it grew cold, after midnight,
He put his arms around me and looped a leg
Over mine and it was nice that way
But I stayed awake with the niceness of it
My sleep stolen by his own deep slumber...
What dreams were lost, I'll never know!
But next morning, just as we'd started breakfast,
A car drew up, and my parents, outraged,
Chastised me for staying out and hustled me home.
Breakfast unfinished. My friend unhappy. My pride wounded.
We met sometimes, but a constraint had grown upon us,
And the following month I heard he'd gone
To an orphanage in Kalimpong.

4

I remember you well, old banyan tree,
As you stood there spreading quietly
Over the broken wall.
While adults slept, I crept away
Down the broad veranda steps, around
The outhouse and the melon-ground...
In that winter of long ago, I roamed
The faded garden of my mother's home.

I must have known that giants have few friends
(The great lurk shyly in their private dens),
And found you hidden by a thick green wall
Of aerial roots.
Intruder in your pillared den, I stood
And shyly touched your old and wizened wood,
And as my heart explored you, giant tree,
I heard you singing!

The spirit of the tree became my friend,
Took me to his silent throbbing heart
And taught me the value of stillness.
My first tutor; friend of the lonely.

And the second was the tonga-man
Whose pony-cart came rattling along the road
Under the furthest arch of the banyan tree.
Looking up, he waved his whip at me
And laughing, called, 'Who lives up there?'
'I do,' I said.
And the next time he came along, he stopped the tonga
And asked me if I felt lonely in the tree.
'Only sometimes,' I said. 'When the tree is thinking.'
'I never think,' he said. 'You won't feel lonely with me.'
And with a flick of the reins he rattled away,
With a promise he'd give me a ride someday.
And from him I learnt the value of promises kept.

5

From the tree to the tonga was an easy drop.
I fell into life. Bansi, tonga-driver,
Wore a yellow waistcoat and spat red
Betel-juice the entire width of the road.
'I can spit further than any man,' he claimed.
It is natural for a man to strive to excel
At something; he spat with authority.

When he took me for rides, he lost a fare.
That was his way. He once said, 'If a girl
Wants five rupees for a fix, bargain like hell
And then give six.'
It was the secret of his failure, he claimed,
To give away more than he owned.
And to prove it, he borrowed my pocket-money
In order to buy a present for his mistress.

A man who fails well is better than one who succeeds badly.

The rattletrap tonga and the winding road
Through the valley, to the river-bed,
With the wind in my hair and the dust
Rising, and the dogs running and barking

And Bansi singing and shouting in my ear,
And the pony farting as it cantered along,
Wheels creaking, seat shifting,
Hood slipping off, the entire contraption
Always about to disintegrate, collapse,
But never quite doing so—like the man himself...
All this was music,
And the ragtime-raga lingers in my mind.

Nostalgia comes swiftly when one is forty,
Looking back at boyhood years.
Even unhappiness acquires a certain glow.

It was shady in the cemetery, and the mango trees
Did well there, nourished by the bones
Of long-dead Colonels, Collectors, Magistrates and Memsahibs.
For here, in dusty splendour, lay the graves
Of those who'd brought their English dust
To lie with Ganges soil: some tombs were temples,
Some were cenotaphs; and one, a tiny Taj.
Here lay sundry relatives, including Uncle Henry,
Who'd been for many years a missionary.
'Sacred to the Memory
Of Henry C. Wagstaff',
Who translated the Gospels into Pashtu,
And was murdered by his own *Chowkidar*.

'Well done, thou good and faithful servant'—
So ran his epitaph.

The gardener, who looked after the trees,
Also dug graves. One day
I found him working at the bottom of a new cavity,
'They never let me know in time,' he grumbled.
'Last week I dug two graves, and now, without warning,
Here's another. It isn't even the season for dying.
There's enough work all summer, when cholera's about—
Why can't they keep alive through the winter?'
Near the railway-lines, watching the trains
(There were six every day, coming or going),
And across the line, the leper colony…
I did not know they were lepers till later
But I knew they were different: some
Were without fingers or toes
And one had no nose
And a few had holes in their faces
And yet some were beautiful
They had their children with them
And the children were no different
From other children.
I made friends with some
And won most of their marbles
And carried them home in my pockets.

One day my parents found me
Playing near the leper colony.
There was a big scene.
My mother shouted at the lepers
And they hung their heads as though it was all their fault,
And the children had nothing to say.
I was taken home in disgrace
And told all about leprosy and given a bath.
My clothes were thrown away
And the servants wouldn't touch me for days.
So I took the marbles I'd won
And put them in my stepfather's cupboard,
Hoping he'd catch leprosy from them.

6

A slim dark youth with quiet
Eyes and a gentle quizzical smile,
Manohar. Fifteen, working in a small hotel.
He'd come from the hills and wanted to return,
I forget how we met
But I remember walking the dusty roads
With this gentle boy, who held my hand
And told me about his home, his mother,
His village, and the little river
At the bottom of the hill where the water

Ran blue and white and wonderful,
'When I go home, I'll take you with me.'
But we hadn't enough money.
So I sold my bicycle for thirty rupees
And left a note in the dining room:
'Going away. Don't worry—(hoping they would)—
I'll come home
When I've grown up.'

We crossed the rushing waters of the Ganga
Where they issued from the doors of Vishnu
Then took the pilgrim road, in those days
Just a stony footpath into the mountains:
Not all who ventured forth returned,
Some came to die, of course,
Near the sacred waters or at their source.
We took this route and spent a night
At a wayside inn, wrapped tight
In the single blanket I'd brought along,
Even then we were cold
It was not the season for pilgrims
And the inn was empty, except for the locals
Drinking a local brew.

We drank a little and listened
To an old soldier from the hills
Talking of the women he'd known
In the first Great War, when stationed in Rome;
His memories were good for many drinks
In many inns; his face pickled in the suns
Of many mountain summers.
The mule-drivers slept in one room
And talked all night over hookahs.
Manohar slept bravely, but I lay watching
A bright star through the tiny window
And wished upon it, already knowing that wishes
Had no power, but wishing all the same...
And next morning we set off again
Leaving the pilgrim-route to march
Down a valley, above a smaller river,
Walking until I felt
We'd walk and walk for ever.
Late at night, on a cold mountain,
Two lonely figures, we saw the lights
Of scattered houses and knew we had arrived.

7

'Not death, but a summing-up of life,'
Said the village patriarch, as we watched him
Treasure a patch of winter sunshine
On his string cot in the courtyard.
I remember his wisdom.
And I remember faces.
For it's faces I remember best.
The people were poor, and the patriarch said:
'I have heard it told that the sun
Sets in splendour in Himalaya—
But who can eat sunsets?'

Perhaps, if I'd stayed longer,
I would have yearned for creature comforts.
We were hungry sometimes, eating wild berries
Or slyly milking another's goat,
Or catching small fish in the river...
But I did not long for home.
Could I have grown up a village boy,
Grazing sheep and cattle, while the Collected Works
Of W. Shakespeare lay gathering dust
In Dehra? Who knows? But it was nice
Of my stepfather to send his office manager
Into the mountains to bring me home!

Manohar.
He called goodbye and waved
As I looked back from the bend in the road.
Bright boy on the mountainside,
Waving to me, calling, and I've loved you
All these years and looked for you everywhere,
In the mountains, in crowds at distant places,
In cities and villages, beside the sea.
And the trains roll on, every day
Hundreds of people coming or going or running away—
Goodbye, goodbye!
Into the forest's silence,
Outside the dark tunnel,
Out of the tunnel, out of the dark...

Secondhand Shop in Hill Station

The smell of secondhand goods
Is everywhere. Lost causes,
Lonely lives, and deaths in small cottages
Among the pines, meet here in the mildewed dark
Of his shop—Abdul Salaam, Proprietor.
Tales of a hundred failures
And ten hundred broken dreams.

A hat-pin and an Iron Cross
Lie down with a blackened pistol,
While a bronze Buddha smiles across
At a plastic doll from Bristol.

Old clothes, old books (perhaps a first edition?),
A dressing-gown, a dagger marked with rust.
A card for some lost Christmas,
And inside, a letter:
'Dear Jane, I am getting better.'
A Chinese vase and a china-dog.

The shop is cold and thick with dust,
The Mall is far from grand;
But Abdul Salaam grows prosperous,
In a suit that's secondhand.

At the Grave of John Mildenhall in Agra

In the year 1594,
Visiting first Lahore
And then the garden city of Ajmer,
Came a merchant adventurer,
John Mildenhall by name,
From London by the River Thame.
To Agra's mart he brought
His goods and baggage, then sought
Audience with the great
Moghul, who sat in state
In a vast red sandstone audience-hall.
'We are pleased, Mr. Mildenhall,
To have you at our court,' great Akbar said;
'Your Queen is known to have an astute head,
Your country many ships, and I hear
Of a poet called Shakespeare—
Who, though not as good as Fazl or Faiz,
Writes a pretty line and does plays on the side.
But tell us—when will you be on your way?'

'Most gracious King, I'd like to stay—
With your permission—for a while,'
Said the traveller with the Elizabethan smile.

To this request the Emperor complied.
John stayed, and settled down, and died.
Over three hundred years had passed
When those who followed, left at last.

WORDS TO LIVE BY

The Wind and the Rain

Like the wind, I run;
Like the rain, I sing;
Like the leaves, I dance;
Like the earth, I'm still;
And in this, Lord, I do thy will.

Pebbles

Pebbles on the seashore.
Millions of pebbles, and yet each one is different.
I pick up a pebble and throw it far out to sea.
For thousands of years the sea will roll over it,
And the pebble will become smoother and rounder,
But after all that time it will still be a pebble,
As you made it, as I threw it.
After all, what is a thousand years?

One Flower

It has bloomed again,
This flower that I thought dead.
In one moment of despair
And pain,
I'd trampled it in the ground
Upon this barren plain.
Little did I know
That it would rise again,
This flower that I thought dead.
My soul would need
A surer weapon than despair
To crush a thing so bright, so fair.

To Live in Magic

What more perfect friend
than the friend you have given me, Lord,
What more perfect song than the
whistling-thrush at dawn's first light,
What lovelier thing than the ladybird
opening its wings on the rose-petal,
What greater gift than this moment in time,
this heart-beat in the night?

For Silence

Thank you, Lord, for silence,
The silence of great mountains
and deserts and forests.
For the silence of the street
late at night
when the last travellers
are safely home
and the traffic is still.
For the silence in my room
in which I can hear small sounds outside:
a moth fluttering against the window pane,
the drip of the dew running off the roof,
and a field mouse rustling through dry leaves.

Last Words

Observing Ananda weeping, Gautama said,
'O Ananda do not weep. This body of ours
contains within itself the powers which renew
its strength for a time, but also the causes which
lead to its destruction. Is there anything put
together which shall not dissolve?'
Then, turning to his disciples, he said, 'When
I am passed away and am no longer with you,
do not think the Buddha has left you, and is not
still in your midst. You have my words, my
explanations, my laws...' And again, 'Beloved
disciples, if you love my memory, love one another.'
And after another pause he said, 'Beloved,
that which causes life causes also decay
and death. Never forget this. I called you to tell you this.'
These were the last words of Gautama
Buddha, as he stretched himself out and died
under the great sal tree, at Kasinagara.

This Land Is Mine

This land is mine
Although I do not own it,
This land is mine
Because I grew upon it.
This dust, this grass,
This tender leaf
And weathered bark
All in my heart are finely blended
Until my time on earth is ended.

Dare to Dream

Build castles in the air
But first, give them foundations.
Hold fast to all your dreams,
Make perfect your creations.

All glory comes to those who dare.

Failed works are sad lame things.
Act impeccably, sing
Your own song, but do not take
Another's song from her or him;
Look for your art within,
You'll find your own true gift,
For you are special too.
And if you try, you'll find
There's nothing you can't do.

Out of the Darkness

Out of darkness we came, into darkness we go,
Out of the sea to the land we know,
Out of the trembling hills and its streams,
From night unto day we come with our dreams.

The wind and the water gave form to our lives;
After thousands of aeons mankind still survives,
And beyond those great spaces, those planets and stars,
Who knows, there are heart-beats and children like ours.

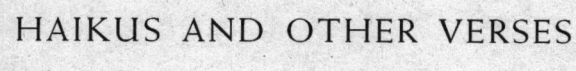

HAIKUS AND OTHER VERSES

Haikus

Whenever I am in a pensive or troubled state, I read (or write) a Haiku. It helps to clear and calm my mind. Here are a few that I wrote last year...

Sweet-scented jasmine in this fold of cloth
I give to you on this your bridal day,
That you forget me not.

There's a begonia in her cheeks,
Pink as the flush of early dawn
On Sikkim's peaks.

Her beauty brought her fame.
But only the wild rose flowering beside her grave
Is there to hear her whispered name.

Bright red
The poinsettia flames
As autumn and the old year wanes.

Petunias I will praise,
Their soft perfume
Takes me by surprise!

The Indian Pink keep flowering without end,
Sturdy and modest,
A loyal friend.

Shaded in a deep ravine,
The ferns stand upright,
Dark and green.

One fine day my kite took wing,
Then came a strong wind—
I was left with the string!

To the temple on the mountain top
We climbed. Forgot to pray!
But got home anyway.

Antirrhinums line the wall,
Sturdy little dragons all!

When I was a boy, I dreamt of
wealth and fame;
And now I'm old, I dream of being
    a boy again.

Jasmine flowers in her hair,
Languid summer days are here,
And sweet longing scents the air.

Out of the Dark

At a ruin upon a hill outside the town
I found some shelter from a summer storm.
An alcove in a wall, moss-green and redolent of bats
But refuge from the wind and rain, an entrance once
To what had been a home, a mansion large and spacious,
Now dream-wrecked, desolate.
And as I stood there, pondering
Upon the mutability of stone, I thought I heard
A haunting cry, insistent on the wind—
'Oh son, please let me in
Oh son, please let me in...'

    Just the soughing of the wind
    In the bending, keening pines;
    Just the rain sibilant on old stones:
    Or was it something more, a voice
    Trapped in the woof of time, imploring still
    And lingering at some door which stood
    Where now I sheltered on a barren hill.

At home, that night, I settled down
To read, the bedlamp on. The night was warm
The storm had passed and all was still outside,
When something, someone, moved about, came tapping on the door.

'Who's there?' I called.
The tapping stopped. And then,
Entreating, came that voice again:

'Oh son, please let me in!'
'Who's there, who's there?' I cried,
And crossed the cold stone floor
Paused for a moment, hand on latch
Then opened wide the door.
Bright moonlight streamed across the sill
And crept along the stair;
I peered outside, to right and left:
Bright road returned my stare.

But long before the dawn, I heard
That tapping once again;
Not on the door this time, but nearer still—
Now rapping quickly on the window-pane.
I lay quite still and held my breath
And thought—surely it's the old oak tree.

Leaves gently tapping on the glass,
Or a moth, or some great beetle winging past.
But through the darkness, pressing in,
As though in me it sought its will,
As though in me it yet would dwell—
'Oh son, please let me in…
Oh, son, please let me in!'

Lost All My Money

I've lost all my money,
And I'm on my way home;
Home to the hills and a field full of rocks.
Nothing in the city but a sickness of the soul,
Nothing to earn but sorrow...
I've lost all my money
And I'm on my way home,
With nothing to buy my way home...
I've lost all my money
And I can't bribe the guard,
So help me, O Lord,
On my way home...

If Mice Could Roar

If mice could roar
And elephants soar
And trees grow up in the sky,
If tigers could dine
On biscuits and wine,
And the fattest of folk could fly!
If pebbles could sing
And bells never ring
And teachers were lost in the post,
If a tortoise could run
And losses be won
And bullies be buttered on toast,
If a song brought a shower
And a gun grew a flower,
This world would be better than most.